GEMS
NATURE'S JEWELS

GARNETS

By Amy Hayes

Gareth Stevens
PUBLISHING

Please visit our website, www.garethstevens.com. For a free color catalog of all our high-quality books, call toll free 1-800-542-2595 or fax 1-877-542-2596.

Library of Congress Cataloging-in-Publication Data

Hayes, Amy, author.
 Garnets / Amy Hayes.
    pages cm. — (Gems : nature's jewels)
 Includes bibliographical references and index.
 ISBN 978-1-4824-2864-3 (pbk.)
 ISBN 978-1-4824-2865-0 (6 pack)
 ISBN 978-1-4824-2866-7 (library binding)
 1. Garnet—Juvenile literature. 2. Precious stones—Juvenile literature. 3. Gems—Juvenile literature. I. Title. II. Series: Gems, nature's jewels.
 QE391.G37H39 2016
 553.8'7—dc23
                                        2015012145

First Edition

Published in 2016 by
Gareth Stevens Publishing
111 East 14th Street, Suite 349
New York, NY 10003

Copyright © 2016 Gareth Stevens Publishing

Designer: Andrea Davison-Bartolotta
Editor: Kristen Rajczak

Photo credits: Cover, pp. 1, 9 (bottom right), 19 Imfoto/Shutterstock.com; p. 4 Art_girl/Shutterstock.com; p. 5 DEA/ PHOTO 1/Getty Images; p. 6 Alina Cardiae Photography/Shutterstock.com; p. 7 Gary Retherford/Getty Images; p. 9 (bottom left) ChinellatoPhoto/Shutterstock.com; p. 9 (top right) Jiri Vaclavek/Shutterstock.com; p. 9 (top left) Manamana/ Shutterstock.com; p. 11 S_E/Shutterstock.com; p. 13 Gary Whitton/Shutterstock.com; p. 15 DEA/L. Douglas/Getty Images; p. 16 Iakov Filimonov/Shutterstock.com; p. 17 © iStockphoto/Gary-UK1; p. 18 Victoria Short/Shutterstock.com; p. 21 (box) Ardely/Shutterstock.com; p. 21 (background) Fletcher & Baylis/Getty Images.

Printed in the United States of America

CPSIA compliance information: Batch #CS15GS: For further information contact Gareth Stevens, New York, New York at 1-800-542-2595.

Contents

Words in the glossary appear in **bold** type the first time they are used in the text.

What Are Garnets?

A garnet isn't just one type of **gem**. Gems called "garnets" are actually part of a group of similar **minerals**. Each of them has a slightly different **chemical** makeup. There are six main types of garnets. The ones most often used are almandine and pyrope.

A garnet is a transparent or translucent crystal. "Transparent" means it can be seen through, and "translucent" means cloudy, but able to let light pass through. Garnets are known for being beautiful red crystals—but they aren't all that color!

Garnet, like many other gems, has to be removed from surrounding rock in order to be used.

Worldwide Gem

Garnets are found all over the world. Garnets are **mined** on every continent, including Antarctica. Many garnets are found in south Asian countries such as Malaysia and Thailand.

Though garnets can be found in **igneous rock**—and less often **sedimentary rock**—they're most commonly found in metamorphic rock. Metamorphic rock is rock that has been changed in some way, by **pressure**, heat, or both. Sometimes garnets are formed when metamorphic rocks move against each other under pressure, too.

Be a Gem Genius!

There might be garnets close to you! There are garnet mines all over Canada and the United States. There are garnet mines in Pennsylvania, Vermont, Connecticut, New York, Idaho, Montana, and more!

What Do Garnets Look Like?

Garnets usually occur as well-formed crystals. They generally have 12 sides or 24 sides.

Because garnets can have several different chemical makeups, they come in many different colors. Garnets are most famous for being a deep red color, but they can also be green, black, yellow, pink, or purple. There are more colors of garnet than there are of any other gem! There are even some garnets that change color in the light.

Be a Gem Genius!

Garnets can be almost any color, but it's **rare** to find a blue garnet.

All colors and kinds of garnets are valued as gems.

Finding a Gem

Garnets are often found in rocks called slate and schist. They're also found in many other kinds of rock, including gneiss and phyllite. Miners also look for garnets in sedimentary sandstone with other minerals such as quartz.

Because garnet is such a common gemstone, many people looking for gold discover garnets among the rocks and gold they find. In fact, garnets are so common that they're only considered **semiprecious** stones. There are even places where families can go to search for their own garnets!

Be a Gem Genius!

The Barton Mine in New York, Garnet Hill Recreaction Area in Nevada, and Morefield Gem Mine in Virginia are all places where you can find garnets!

A garnet can be a mix of the main kinds of the garnet family of minerals. It might be 70 percent almandine, 20 percent grossular, and 10 percent pyrope, for example.

Garnet Mining

Garnets are mined in a few ways. In some areas, garnets are trapped in hard rock, and lots of work is done digging huge holes called open-pit mines to get them out. Garnets are also found in streams, and miners use big screens called sifters to find them.

Garnets are heavy, so it's easy to separate them from dirt and other rocks by putting them in water. Garnets will fall to the bottom of the water the fastest, while other rocks will float on top.

Be a Gem Genius!

Most garnets aren't mined to be gems! Garnets are very hard, so they're often ground down to use for sandpaper.

Many gemstones and other valuable minerals are mined in open-pit mines like this one.

Choosing a Gem

Once garnets have been separated from other rocks and dirt, those that would be good for **jewelry** are chosen. Some natural garnet formations are very beautiful but wouldn't make good gems. They could be too dark in color or have flaws or fracture lines. Fracture lines may mean a garnet could break easily.

Every stone is looked at carefully and tapped lightly to see if it will break apart. The biggest, nicest garnets go to a lapidary, or gem cutter.

Be a Gem Genius!

Fracture is one property of minerals. It's the mark left when a mineral is chipped or broken. Fracture can take many forms, including uneven, crumbly, or smooth, depending on the gem.

Garnets have to be flawless in order to be used as gemstones.

Making Garnet Jewelry

To make a garnet ready to be used for jewelry, it needs to be cut. The lapidary first takes the garnet and dunks it in water. Then, he shapes the garnet into the right size. After that, the lapidary sands the garnet, creates **facets**, and removes any scratches.

Finally, the garnet is polished, meaning all its sides are made smooth. It's ready to become a part of a beautiful bracelet or other piece of jewelry.

In order to shape and polish stones well,
lapidaries must practice using special tools.

What Makes Garnets Valuable?

Not many garnets are valuable, and most of them certainly aren't as valuable as emeralds, rubies, or other rare stones. But what makes some garnets more valuable than others?

All stones are valued based on their size, color, **clarity**, and cut. Garnets are more valuable if they're an unusual color because these garnets have an uncommon chemical makeup. Green garnets called tsavorite aren't found often and neither are orange spessartite garnets or pink rhodolite garnets. Color-changing garnets are some of the least often found.

spessartite garnet

Spessartite garnets are known for their brilliance.
For colored gems, having "brilliance" means light
bounces off the inside of the gem, making it seem
like it's even more colorful!

Really Rare Garnets

The rarest of all garnets is the blue garnet. In fact, it wasn't even discovered until the late 1990s. The blue-green garnet was found only in Bekily, Madagascar. The unusual blue color is caused by large amounts of the element vanadium in the stone.

Madagascar blue garnets are actually color-changing garnets that change from blue-green in daylight to purple in light from lamps or light bulbs. They're worth $1.5 million per carat (0.007 oz)!

Be a Gem Genius!

There are only a few kinds of gems that change color in the light, such as some kind of sapphires!

Glittering Garnets

- Egyptian pharaohs were buried with garnet necklaces to wear in the afterlife.

- "Carbuncle" is an old name for garnets.

- Explorers and travelers used to carry garnets with them. The gems were supposed to light up the night and keep travelers safe.

- Red garnets have been ground up as medicine to treat heart and blood illnesses.

- Native Americans used garnets as bullets in guns.

Glossary

chemical: matter that can be mixed with other matter to cause changes

clarity: the state of being clear

facet: a small, flat area on a jewel

gem: a stone of some value that is cut and shaped

igneous rock: the rock that forms when hot, liquid rock from within Earth rises and cools

jewelry: pieces of metal, often holding gems, worn on the body

mine: to remove rocks or other matter from a pit or tunnel. Also, the pit or tunnel from which rocks and other matter are taken.

mineral: matter in the ground that forms rocks

pressure: a force that pushes on something else

rare: uncommon or special

sedimentary rock: the rock that forms when sand, stones, and other matter are pressed together over a long time

semiprecious: having to do with minerals that may be used as gems but aren't as valuable as other gemstones

For More Information

Books

Squire, Ann O. *Gemstones.* New York, NY: Children's Press, 2013.

Symes, R. F. *Eyewitness Rocks & Minerals.* New York, NY: DK Publishing, 2014.

Websites

Garnet
geology.com/minerals/garnet.shtml
See pictures of many different colors of garnet, and read more about
the gem.

GemKids: Gem Explorer
gemkids.gia.edu/view-all-gemstones
Learn about all kinds of gems here!

Gems – Mineral Crystals
www.kidsgeo.com/geology-for-kids/0025A-gems.php
How are gems created? Find out on this website for kids.

Index